IGUANODON

the DINOSAUR with the...

fat bottom

Helen Greathead
Illustrated by Mike Spoor

SCHOLASTIC

Professor Michael J Benton – dinosaur consultant
Valerie Wilding – educational advisor
Ben Newth – researcher

Scholastic Children's Books,
Commonwealth House, 1-19 New Oxford Street,
London WC1A 1NU, UK

A division of Scholastic Ltd
London ~ New York ~ Toronto ~ Sydney ~ Auckland
Mexico City ~ New Delhi ~ Hong Kong

Published in the UK by Scholastic Ltd, 2003

Text copyright © Helen Greathead, 2003
Illustrations copyright © Mike Spoor, 2003

ISBN 0 439 98284 7

All rights reserved
Printed and bound by Nørhaven Paperback A/S, Denmark

2 4 6 8 10 9 7 5 3 1

The right of Helen Greathead and Mike Spoor to be identified as author and illustrator of this work respectively has been asserted by them in accordance with the Copyright, Designs and Patents Act, 1988.

This book is sold subject to the condition that it shall not, by way of trade or otherwise be lent, resold, hired out, or otherwise circulated without the publisher's prior consent in any form of binding or cover other than that in which it is published and without a similar condition, including this condition, being imposed on a subsequent purchaser.

Contents

Introduction **5**

Iguanodon has a bite to eat **6**

Iguanodon gets into a fight **22**

Iguanodon lays some eggs **40**

Iguanodon is discovered **50**

Introduction

Dinosaur names are often hard to say. It's easier to say them in bits:

Ig-wah-nerd-on

Say it slowly, then say it faster. Now you'll remember how to say Iguanodon!

Iguanodon has a bite to eat

A lot of dinosaurs had fat bottoms. Iguanodon didn't have the fattest bottom of all, but have a look:

Iguanodon bottom

Your bottom

It is big, isn't it?

Why did Iguanodon need such a fat bottom?

Was it nice to sit on?

Oof!

Was it good for bumping other dinosaurs out of the way?

Was it because Iguanodon was a greedy dinosaur?

Nobody knows for sure.

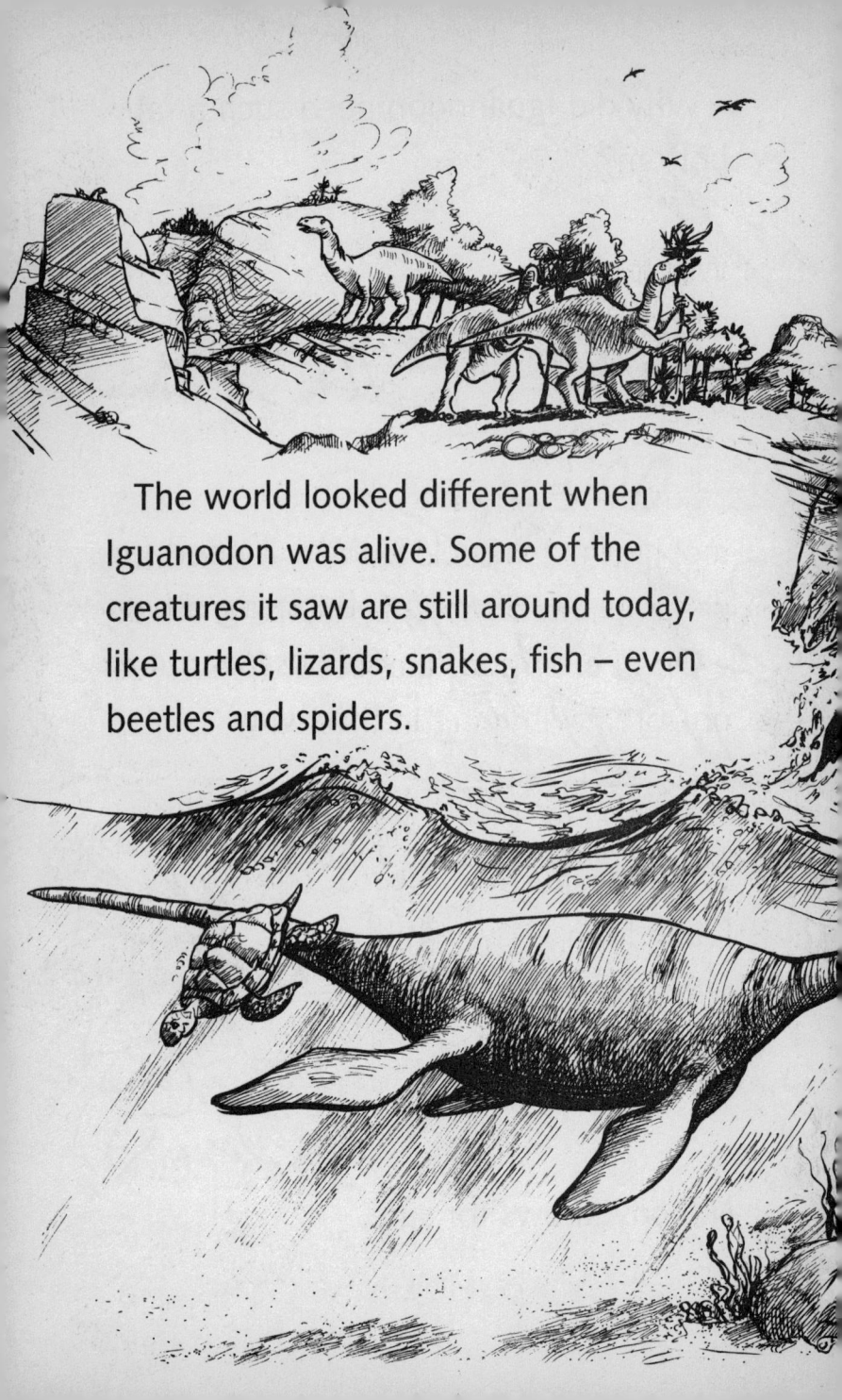

The world looked different when Iguanodon was alive. Some of the creatures it saw are still around today, like turtles, lizards, snakes, fish – even beetles and spiders.

But there were lots of other dinosaurs, too! Iguanodon could look up to see a huge pterosaur (ter-oh-sore) flying across the sky. Or an enormous plesiosaur (please-ee-oh-sore) swimming in the sea.

Dinosaurs came in all shapes and sizes, from little Hypsilophodon (hip-sil-oaf-oh-don), to absolutely enormous Brachiosaurus (brack-ee-oh-sore-us).

There were huge forests with very tall trees. The biggest dinosaurs were so big, they ripped up whole trees for food! And when the sun shone on the forest floor, smaller plants started to grow.

Iguanodon probably saw some of the first flowers *ever* …

… and ate them!

Yes, Iguanodon was a vegetarian dinosaur. It didn't eat meat.

Iguanodon had to make do with leaves, ferns, plants, even small trees – and maybe some fruits and seeds if it was lucky!

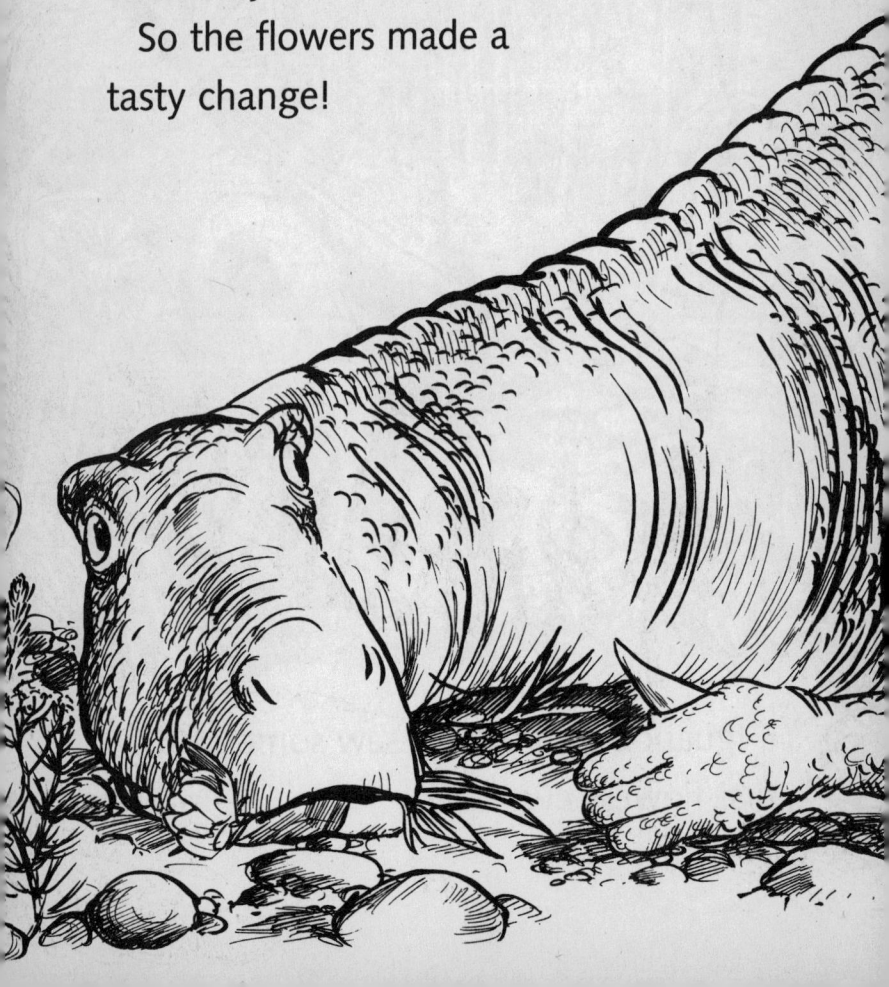

So the flowers made a tasty change!

The leaves that grew millions of years ago were tough. Really tough. Iguanodon probably had lots of tummy aches.

RRRUMBLE

1 Iguanodon needed a big tummy to cope with all the food it ate.

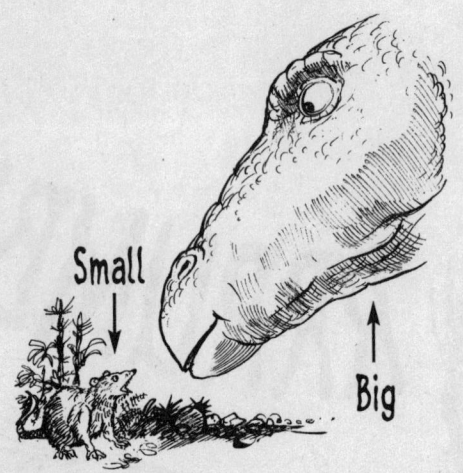

2 Because it had a big tummy it was a big dinosaur.

3 And because it was a big dinosaur, it had to keep eating nearly all the time.

4 It needed a big, fat bottom to balance that big, fat tummy!

Parp!

To get down to some serious eating, Iguanodon had to get comfortable. It rested on its chunky back legs and used its stiff, straight tail to prop itself up (a bit like having a stool stuck to your bottom!).

Instead of front teeth it had a sort of beak. The beak nipped off the tasty green leaves and shoots, leaving behind the twiggy bits. Iguanodon chewed the greens with its back teeth and swallowed them into that enormous tum.

Beak

Scientists think dinosaur teeth are really exciting. Teeth tell them all sorts of things about a dinosaur.

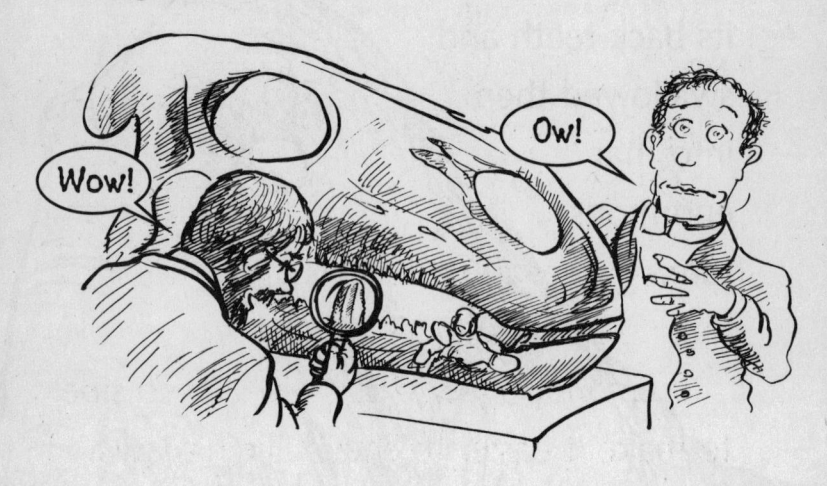

They know Iguanodon was a vegetarian because its teeth weren't strong enough to cut into meat.

Iguanodon's teeth looked like this:

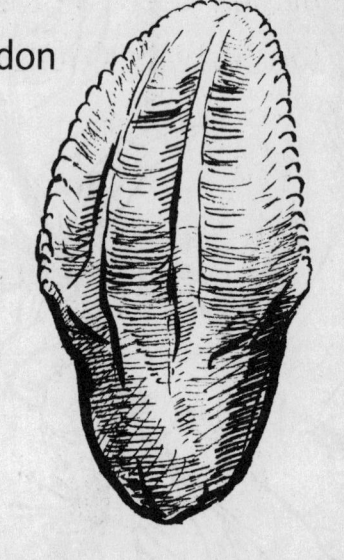

They were good for chewing, not for ripping other animals to bits!

Iguanodon's jaws slid from side to side to make it easier to chew. Sliding jaws helped keep the teeth nice and sharp, too. Which is quite clever really!

Bad news: a dinosaur that ate a lot had to poo a lot. Maybe four times a day! A good use for that fat bottom!

Good news: the poos didn't smell as bad as you think. And they were good for the plants!

Seeds that Iguanodon ate with its dinner …

Seeds

… came out again when it pooed …

… so more plants grew.

Poo

Iguanodon gets into a fight

Seeing Iguanodon chomping its way through the forest would be scary, wouldn't it? Iguanodon wouldn't hurt you, though ... as long as you kept out of the way! And that's just what a lot of creatures did.

They kept out of Iguanodon's way because it *looked* big and scary. Another good reason for having a fat bottom! Iguanodon could use it – and the rest of its body to frighten other animals.

Sometimes Iguanodon did get nasty. It could protect itself with the help of its amazing hands. Each one was like a hand and a foot all in one! And they were a bit different from yours. Have a look:

Iguanodon hand

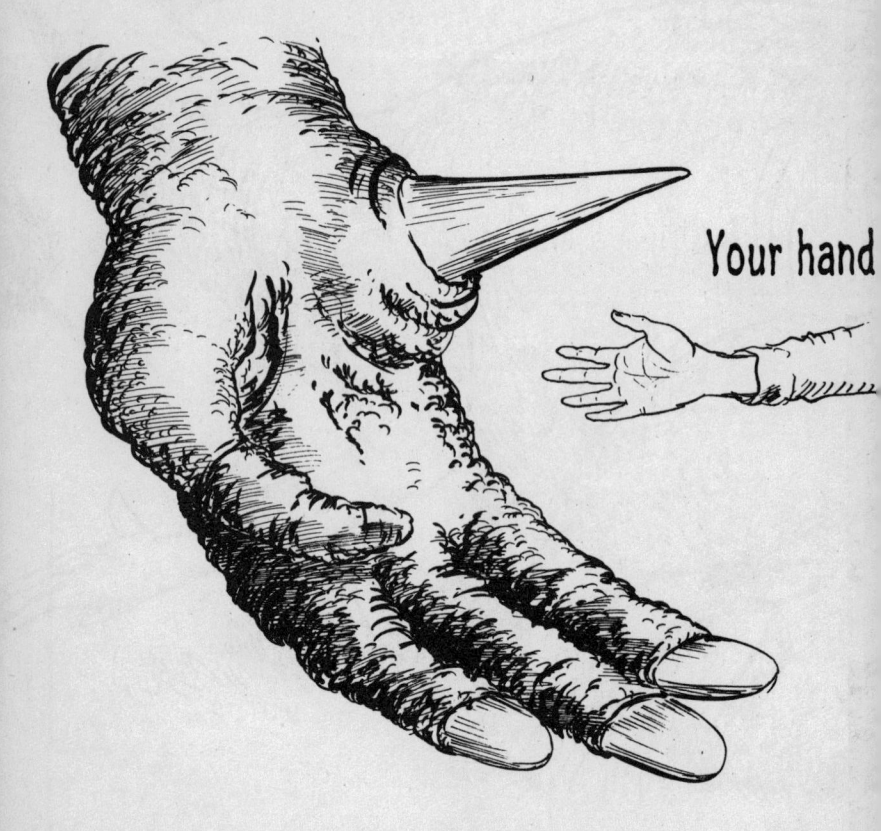

Your hand

What could you do if your hands looked like this?

- A handstand – easy!

- Open a can with your thumb!

- Have a really good scratch – careful, that spike's sharp!

The three middle fingers on Iguanodon's hand worked more like toes:

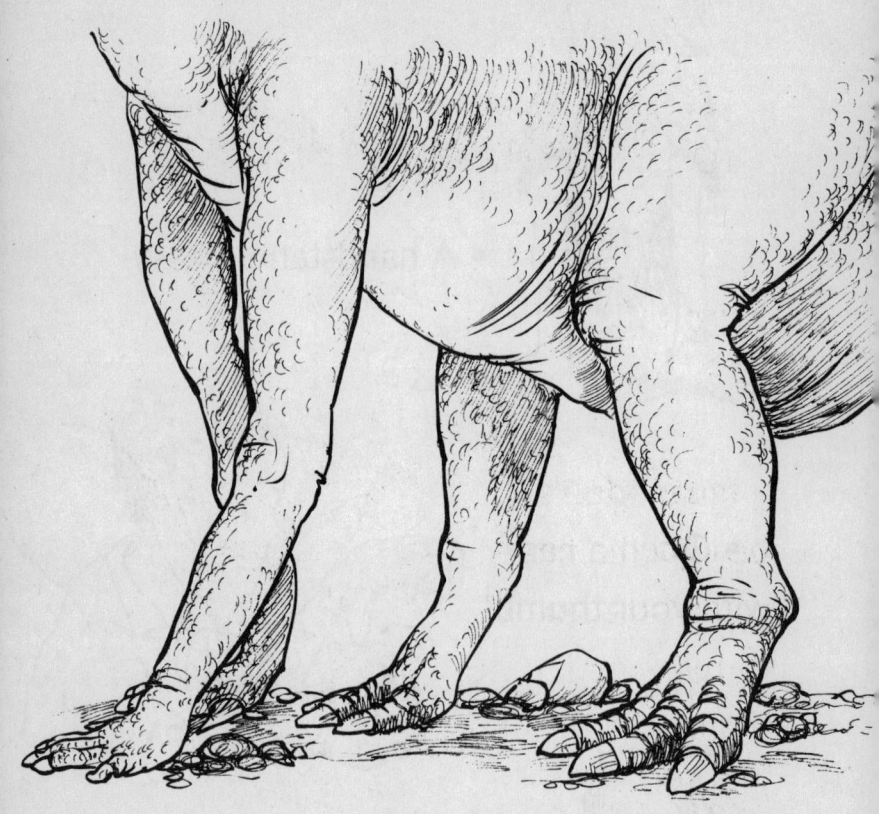

Iguanodon walked and ran on its legs, but it could use its arms too, for standing or resting. Sometimes it walked on all fours, especially when it was looking for food.

Standing still

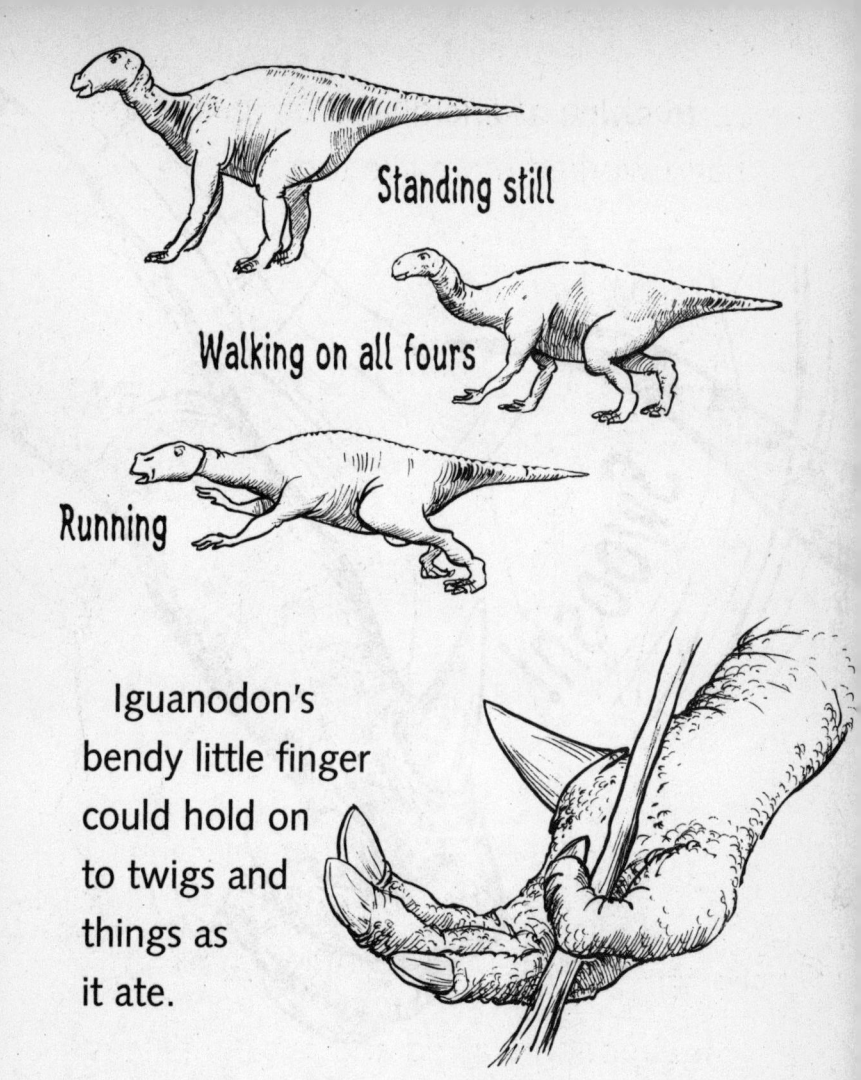

Walking on all fours

Running

Iguanodon's bendy little finger could hold on to twigs and things as it ate.

And then there was the spike! It was great for breaking open seed pods and fruits, but there was another good use for it …

... to swipe at enemies!

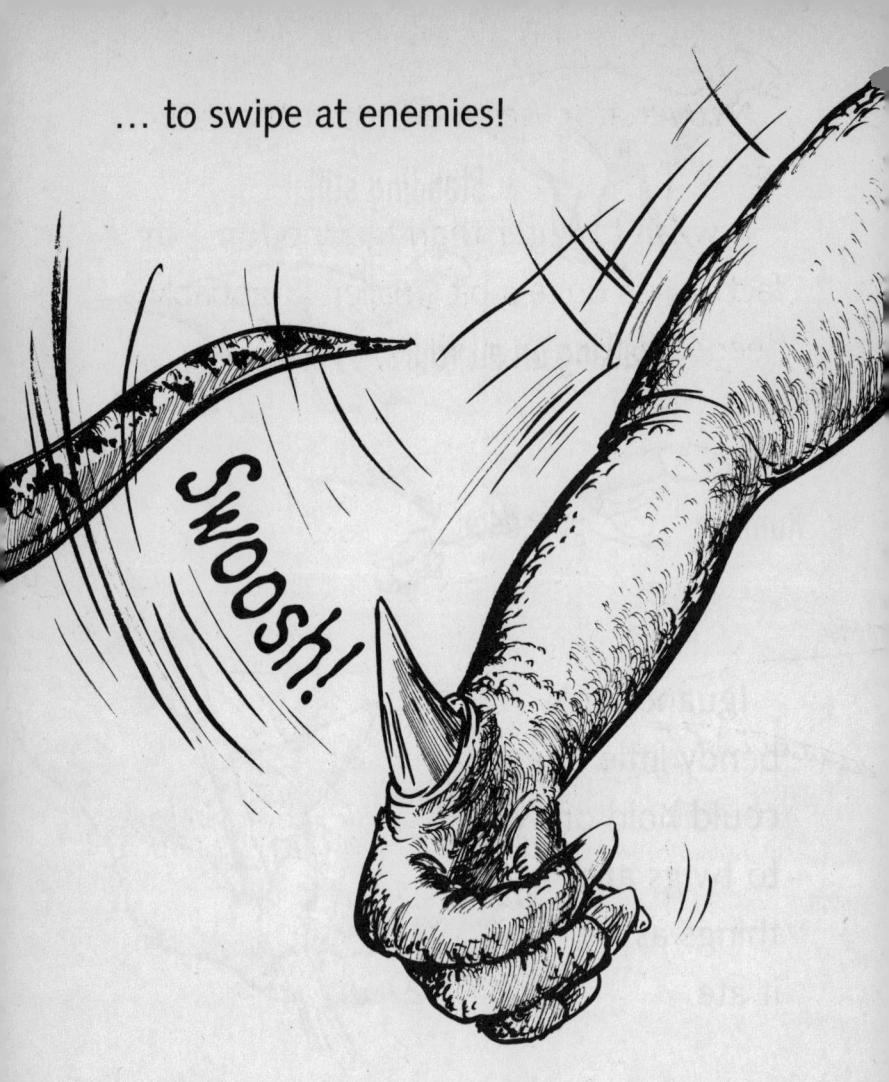

Swoosh!

Even though Iguanodon was huge, some other dinosaurs thought it might be a tasty meal. Neovenator (knee-oh-venner-tor) was one of them.

Neovenator was a dinosaur that ate meat.

It wasn't bigger than Iguanodon – in fact, it was quite a bit smaller. It probably needed a friend to help it attack.

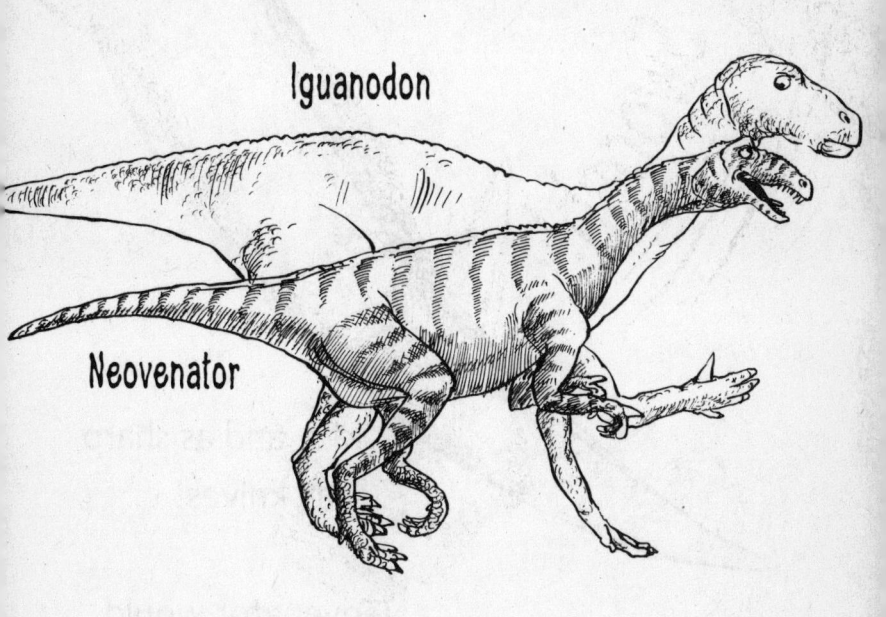

Iguanodon

Neovenator

Neovenator ran on two legs, like Iguanodon. It also had a long tail, like Iguanodon. But its bottom wasn't nearly so fat and …

… Neovenator had great big legs, so it could run even faster than you. It had nasty, sharp claws on its fingers.

And you wouldn't want to go near those teeth!

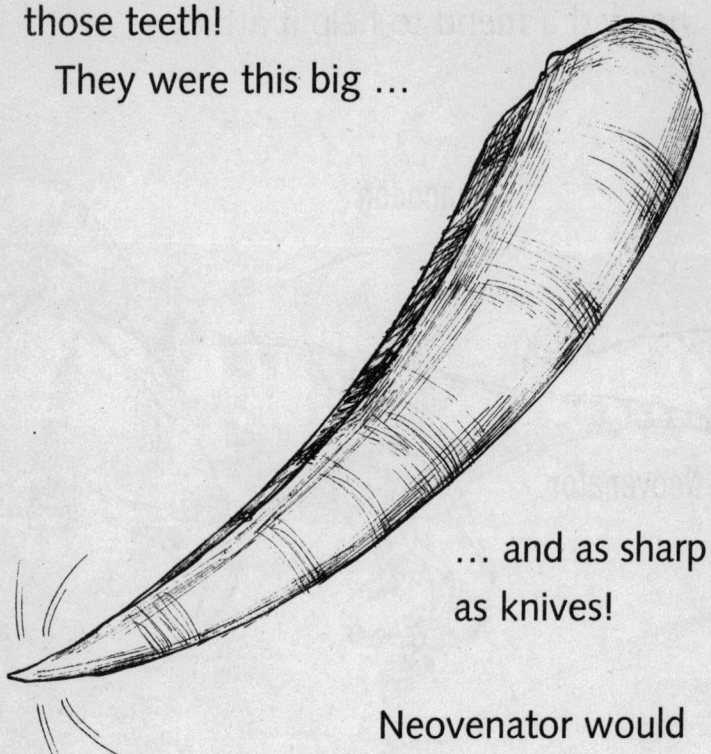

They were this big …

… and as sharp as knives!

Neovenator would jump out at Iguanodon, jaws open, ready to bite! It would try to use its claws to stop Iguanodon running away.

But Iguanodon could fight back. Jabbing its thumb spike into Neovenator's eye or throat. Nasty!

Then there was Baryonyx (barry-on-ics). Some scientists found a Baryonyx skeleton near some Iguanodon bones.

They thought Baryonyx liked to hunt and eat Iguanodons.

Baryonyx had jaws a bit like a crocodile. It walked on two legs and had a huge hook on its hand. The hook was sharp and deadly. An easy match for Iguanodon's thumb spike.

So did Baryonyx and Iguanodon fight? Other scientists say this is rubbish. Baryonyx only ate Iguanodons that were already dead. This means Baryonyx was a "scavenger", not a killer.

The scientists think Baryonyx lived near water. Its big hands, its claws and even its crocodile mouth were just right for catching fish.

And fishing was a lot easier than fighting Iguanodon!

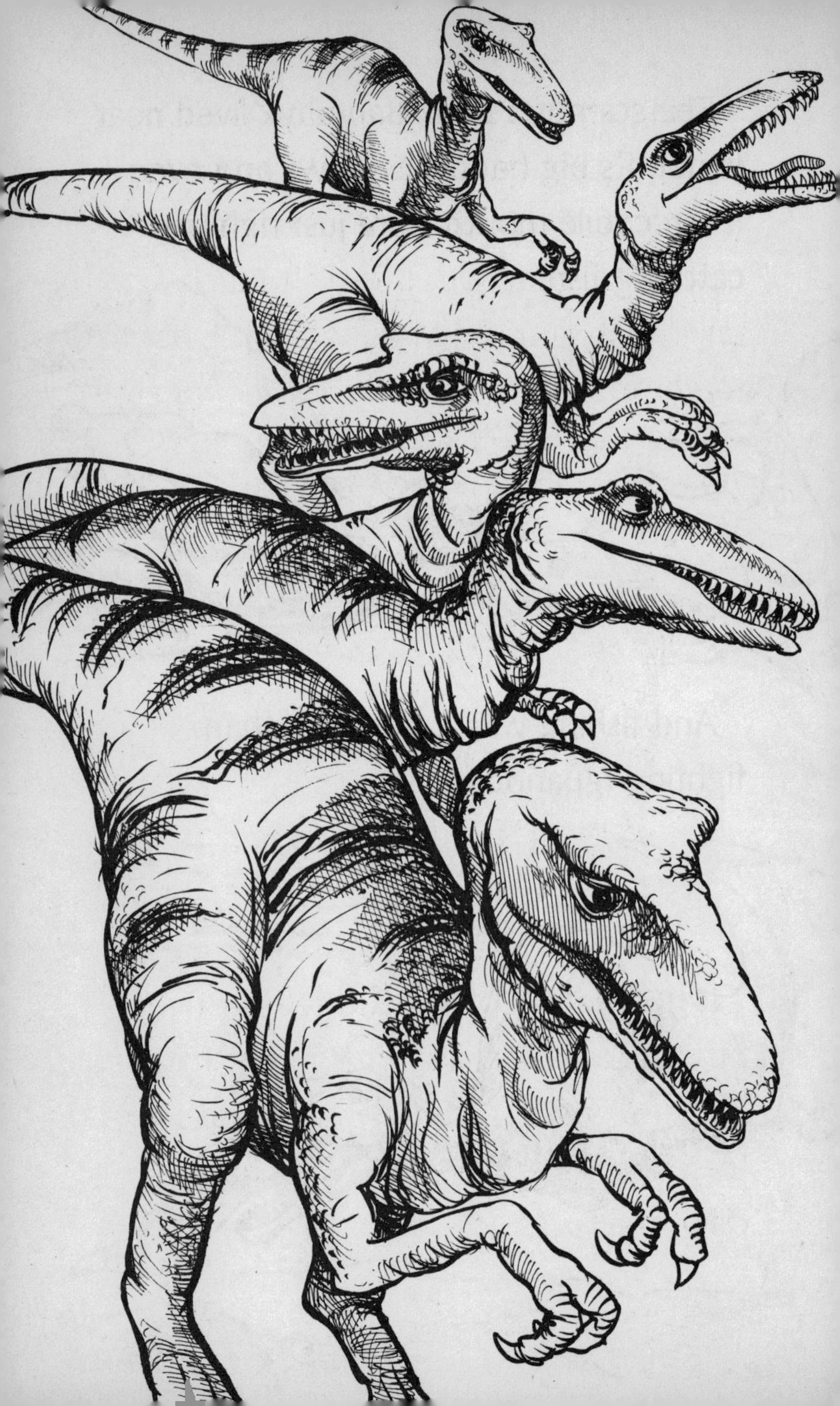

Being a great big Iguanodon wasn't enough to scare off all small dinosaurs.

Deinonychus (die-none-eek-us) had quite a long tail, but it wasn't much taller than you. And you wouldn't want to get too close! Deinonychus definitely *wasn't* friendly!

It hunted in a gang with four or five others. Together, they could hunt for bigger dinosaurs. Deinonychus had sharp teeth and killer claws, too. The nastiest claw of all was …

... on his foot!

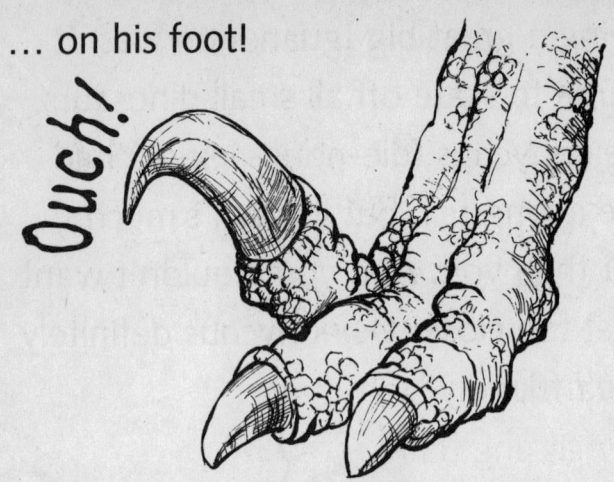

Ouch!

The Deinonychus gang jumped on Iguanodon. Then, balancing on one leg, they used the other to jab their killer toe claws into Iguanodon's tum.

Iguanodon fought back by whacking them away with its huge tail ...

... kicking its big back legs ...

Hurray!

... or using its fat bottom – to squash them!

Iguanodon lays some eggs

Life for Iguanodons wasn't all eating and fighting. They had babies, too!

No one has ever seen an Iguanodon egg, but scientists think the mum made a nest and laid them. Iguanodon was a bit big to nest up a tree! Instead it used its arms to dig a nest from soft, dry earth. It looked like this…

... and held 20 or 30 eggs. (Imagine all those brothers and sisters!) But the eggs were a tasty treat for lizards and small, hungry dinosaurs. So laying lots of eggs meant at least a few would hatch and survive.

Slurp!

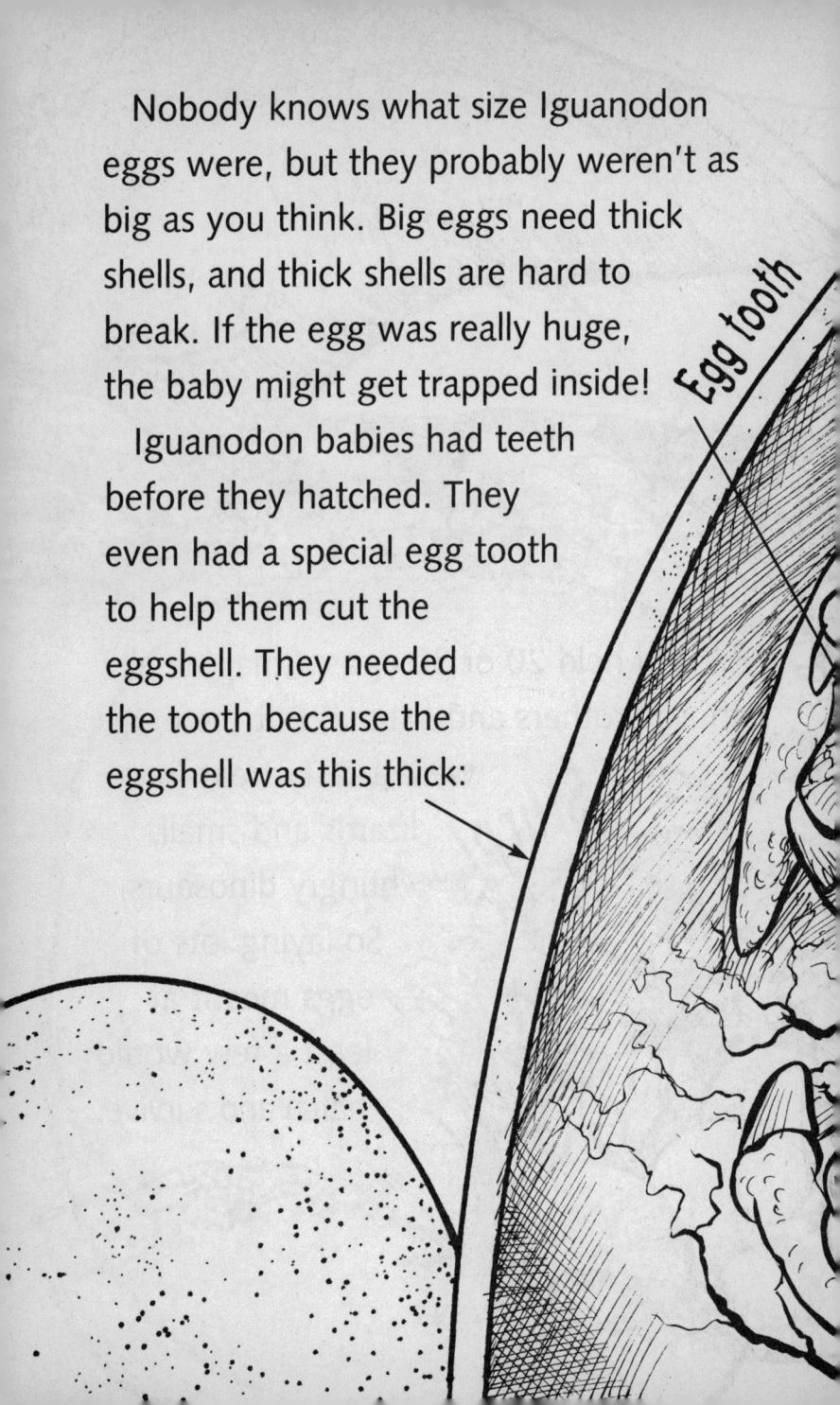

Nobody knows what size Iguanodon eggs were, but they probably weren't as big as you think. Big eggs need thick shells, and thick shells are hard to break. If the egg was really huge, the baby might get trapped inside!

Iguanodon babies had teeth before they hatched. They even had a special egg tooth to help them cut the eggshell. They needed the tooth because the eggshell was this thick:

Egg tooth

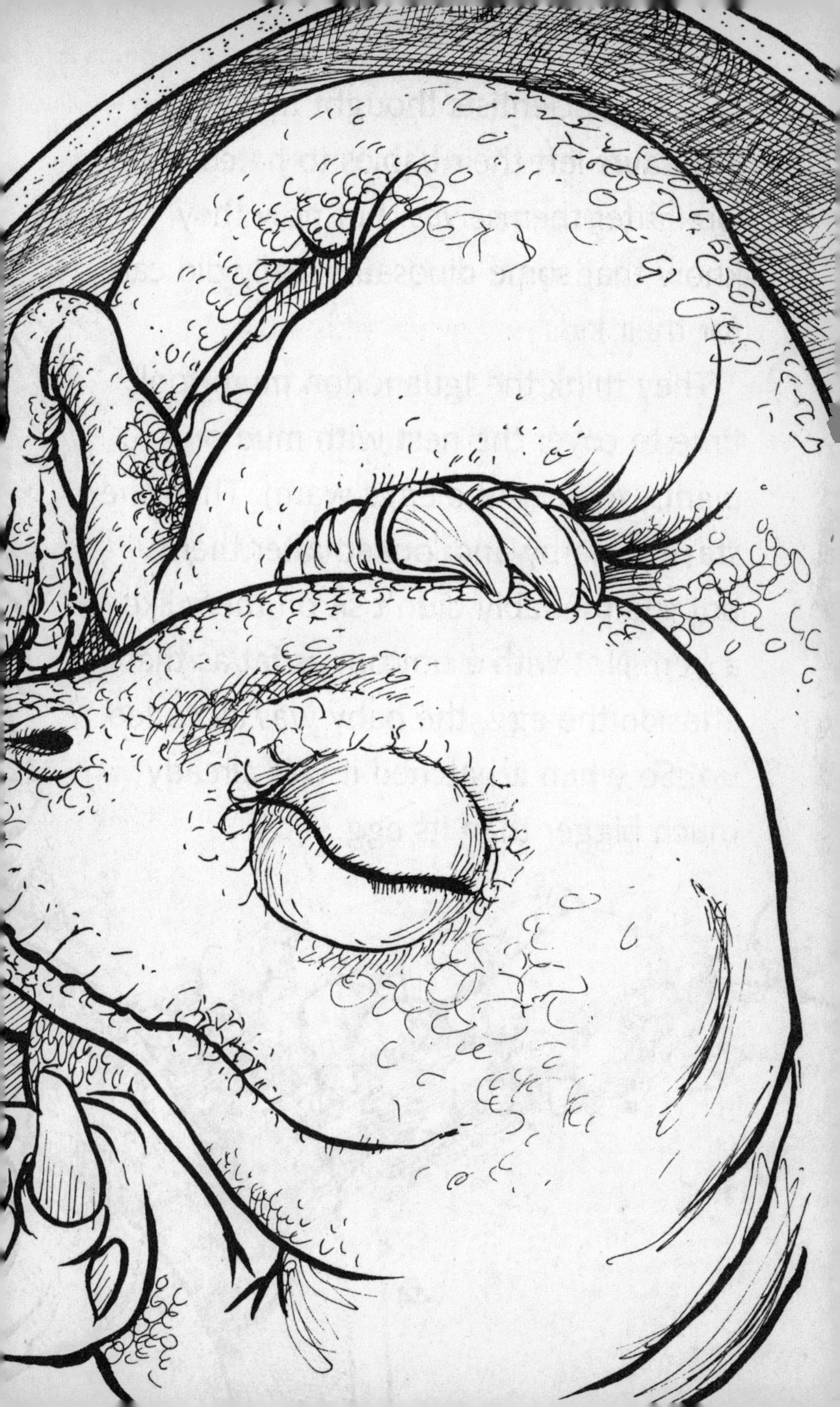

At first, scientists thought that dinosaurs left their babies to hatch and look after themselves. But now they know that some dinosaurs really did care for their kids.

They think the Iguanodon mum took time to cover the nest with mud or plants, to keep the eggs warm. Then she stayed nearby and looked after them, but she probably didn't sit on them like a hen. Not with a bottom as fat as that!

Inside the egg, the baby was all curled up! So when it hatched it was already much bigger than its egg.

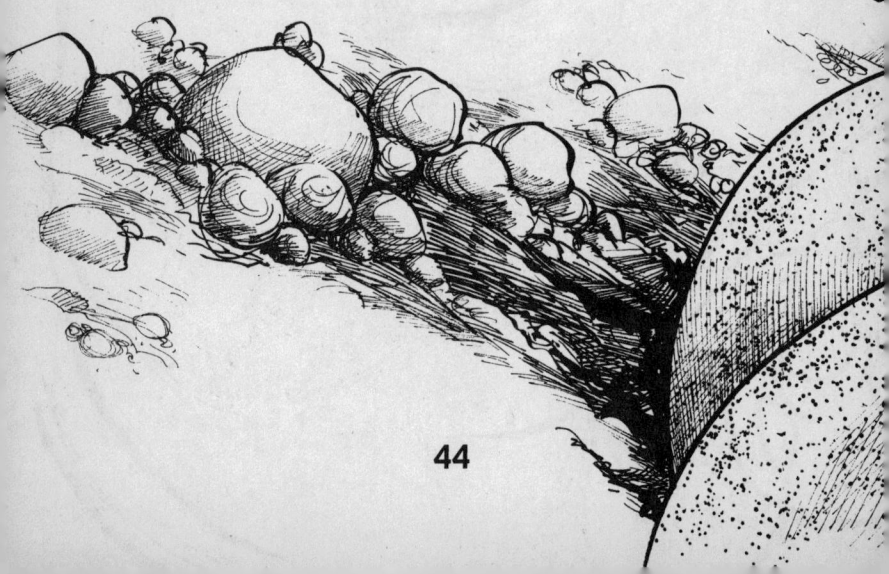

45

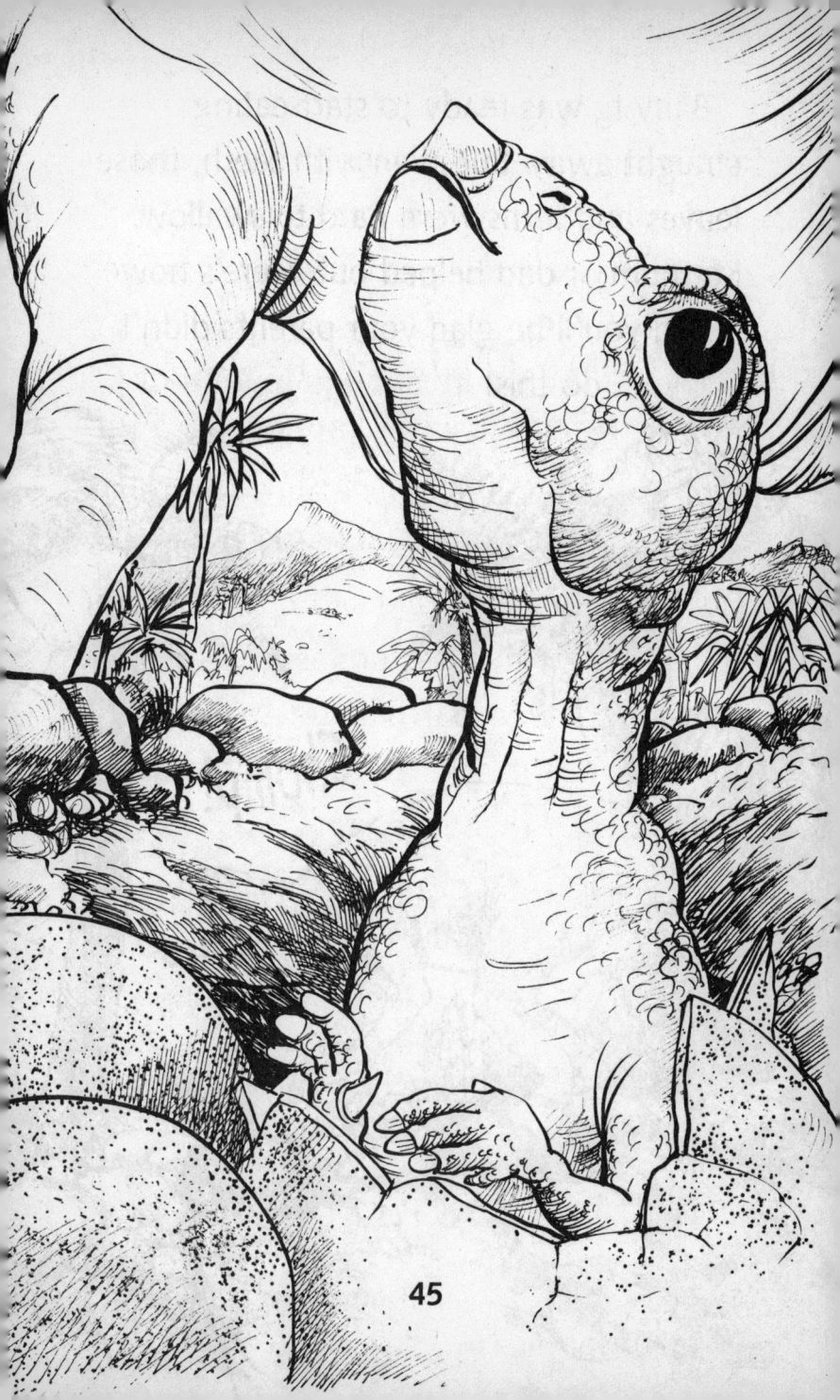

Baby Ig was ready to start eating straight away. But even with teeth, those leaves and ferns were hard to swallow. So mum or dad helped out. Here's how – and you'll be glad your parents didn't do this!

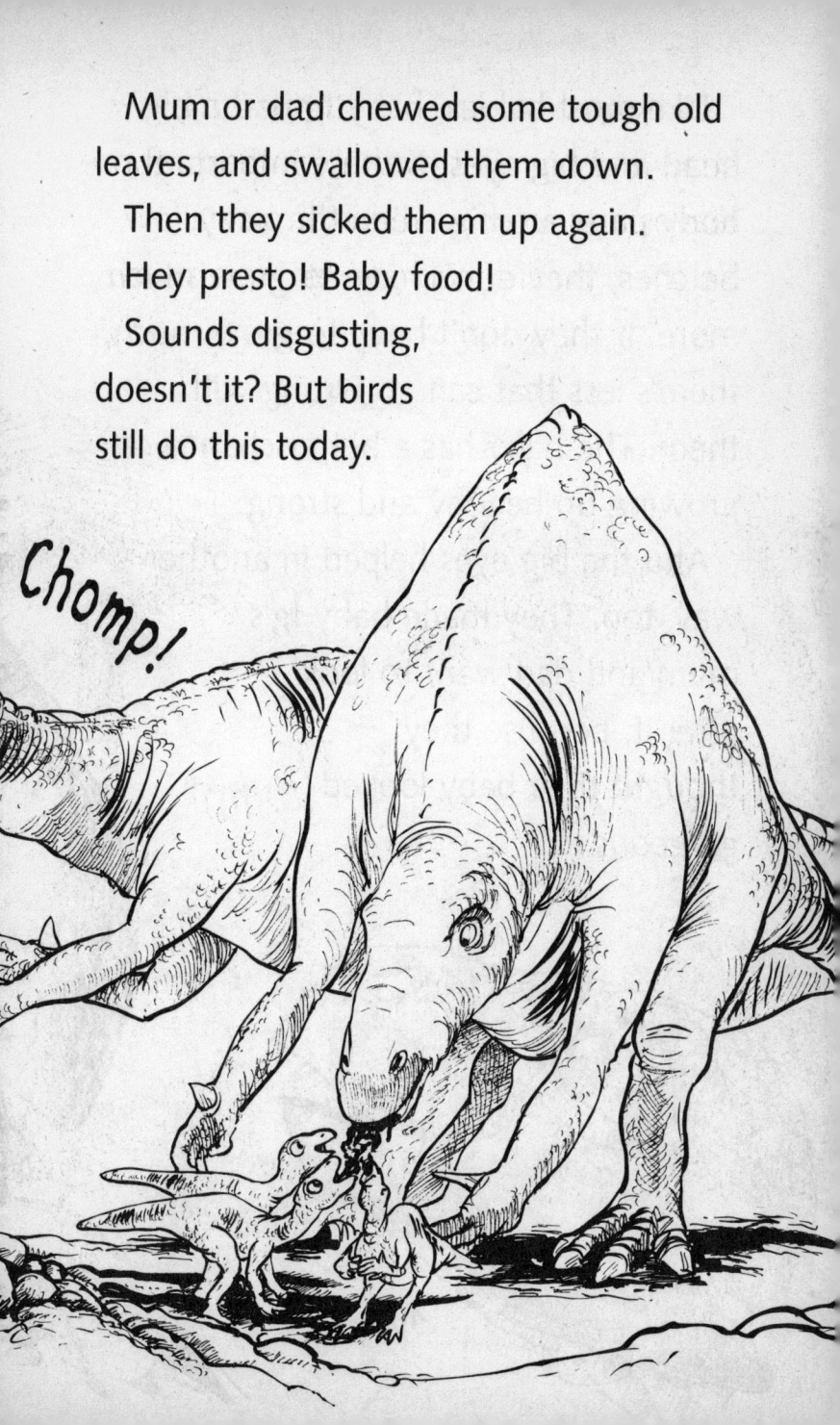

Mum or dad chewed some tough old leaves, and swallowed them down.

Then they sicked them up again.

Hey presto! Baby food!

Sounds disgusting, doesn't it? But birds still do this today.

Chomp!

Like most babies, baby Ig had a big head and big eyes. If these important body parts are big when the baby hatches, they don't have to grow much more. If they don't have to grow much, there's less that can go wrong with them. The baby has a better chance of growing up healthy and strong.

And the big eyes helped in another way, too. They made baby Ig's mum and dad want to look after it, because they thought their baby looked *gorgeous*.

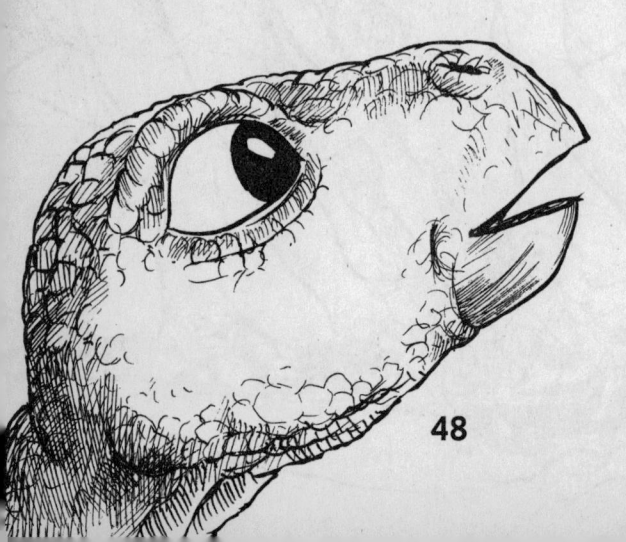

Ahhhh!

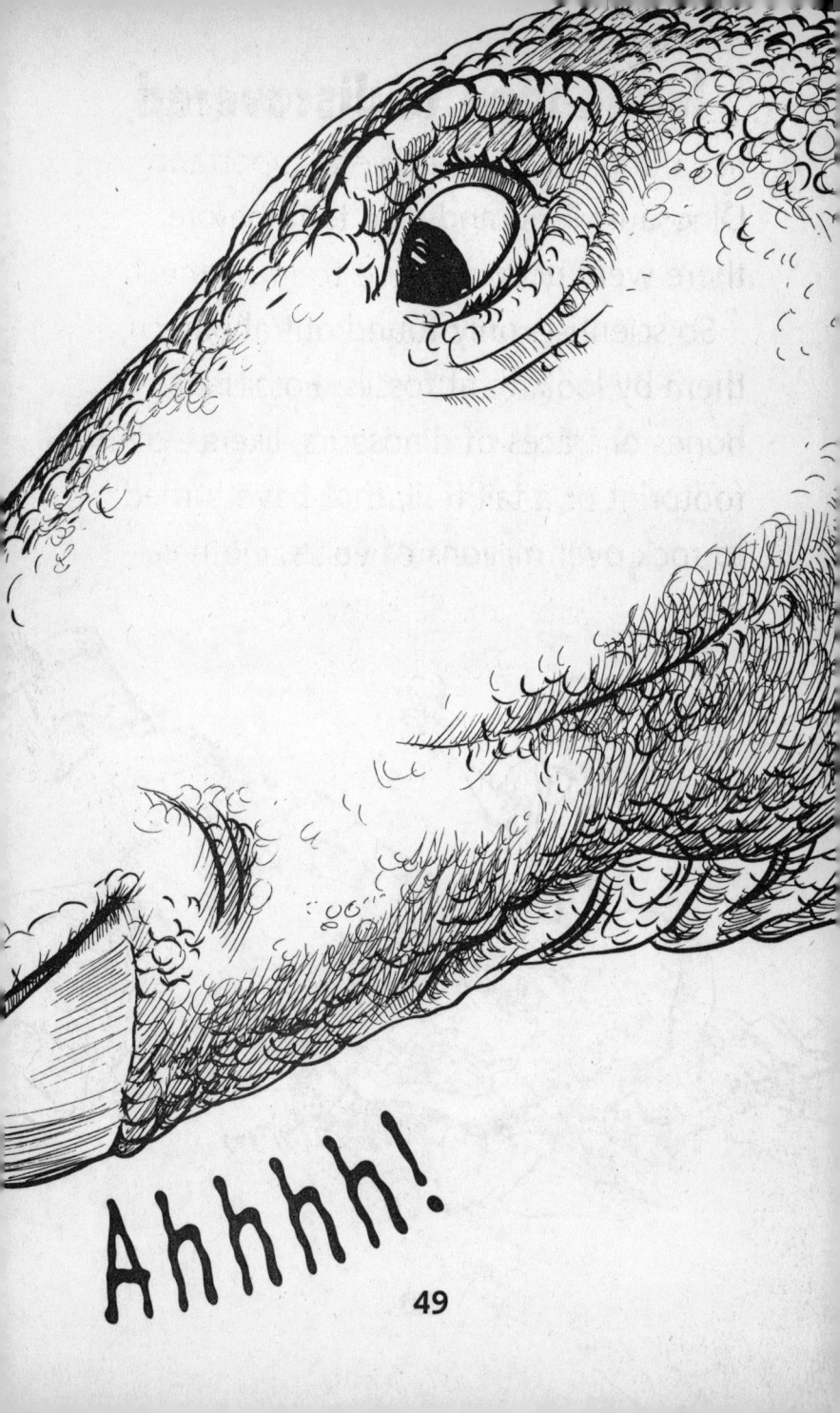

Iguanodon is discovered

Dinosaurs lived and died long before there were people.

So scientists only found out about them by looking at fossils. Fossils are bones or traces of dinosaurs, like a footprint or a tail trail, that have turned to rock over millions of years.

People didn't always know what fossils were. The first scientists to discover fossilized dinosaur bones found that not many people believed them!

An English Doctor, called Gideon Mantell, discovered Iguanodon over 150 years ago. Dr Mantell's hobby was fossil hunting. He spent all his spare time searching in the woods near his home.

Dig

Chip

Hmm?

Phew!

One day he came across a different sort of fossil. It looked like a tooth! A very strange tooth. He knew it belonged to a very unusual creature.

Very interesting.

Dr Mantell thought the tooth came from some sort of giant lizard. But other scientists laughed at him. They said the tooth was from:

An elephant!

A rhinoceros!

A big fish!

Dr Mantell set out to prove the scientists wrong.

He searched through drawers and drawers of lizard and snake skeletons. Creepy!

And he found something! His fossil tooth was just like the tooth of an iguana. That's a modern type of lizard.

But the fossil tooth was 20 times bigger. This was quite some lizard!

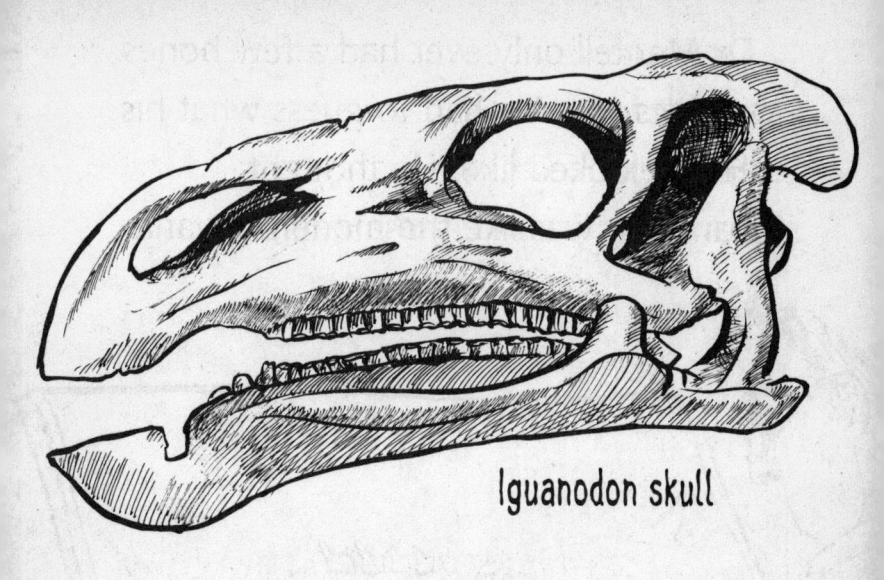

Iguanodon skull

Iguana skull

Dr Mantell called the creature Iguanodon. Which means "iguana tooth". And he wrote about it, saying that giant reptiles once walked the forests of southern England.

People stopped laughing and started to listen to him.

Dr Mantell only ever had a few bones to work from. He had to guess what his creature looked like. He thought Iguanodon was like the modern iguana:

Other scientists had different ideas. They thought the creature was more like a rhinoceros, with four huge legs and a very fat bottom!

Can you see what happened to the thumb spike? They all put it on the end of Iguanodon's nose!

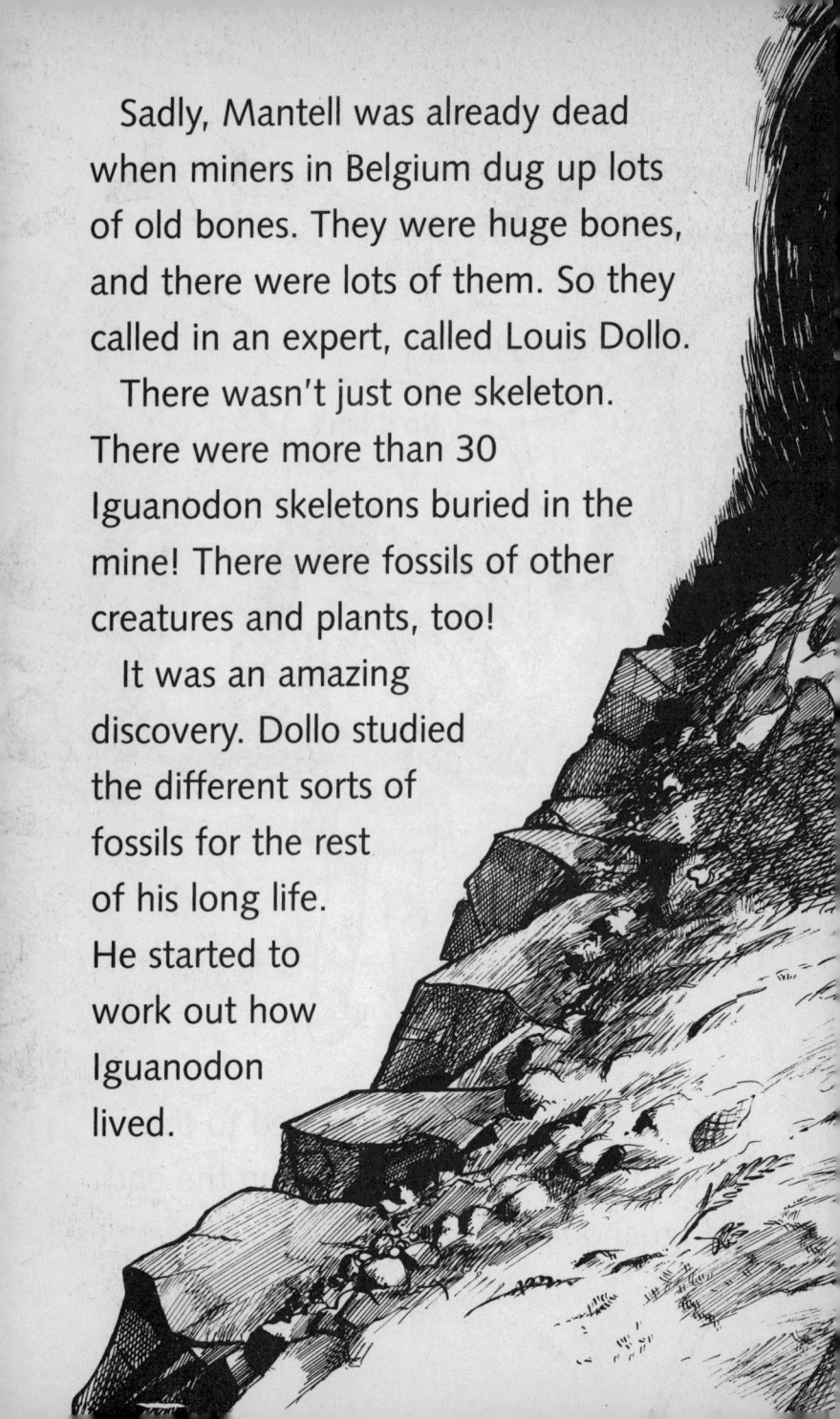

Sadly, Mantell was already dead when miners in Belgium dug up lots of old bones. They were huge bones, and there were lots of them. So they called in an expert, called Louis Dollo.

There wasn't just one skeleton. There were more than 30 Iguanodon skeletons buried in the mine! There were fossils of other creatures and plants, too!

It was an amazing discovery. Dollo studied the different sorts of fossils for the rest of his long life. He started to work out how Iguanodon lived.

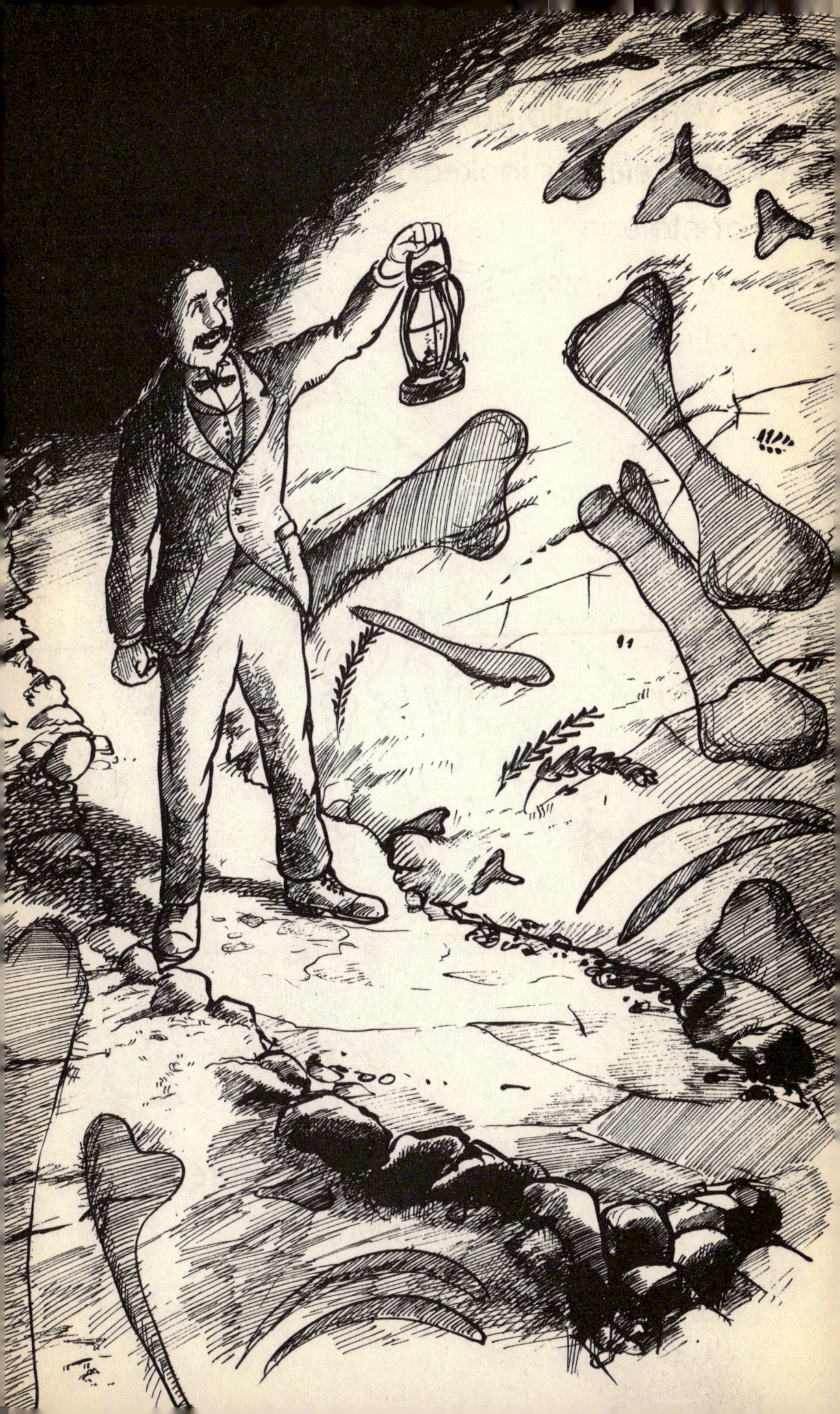

When Dollo put the bones together, the skeletons looked like this:

He thought Iguanodon was more like a kangaroo than a rhinoceros!

And Dollo found out loads about Iguanodon. Lots of the things he discovered are things you've read about in this book:

- It definitely walked on two legs.
- Its arms were used for grasping food.
- It had *two* spikes, one on each thumb!

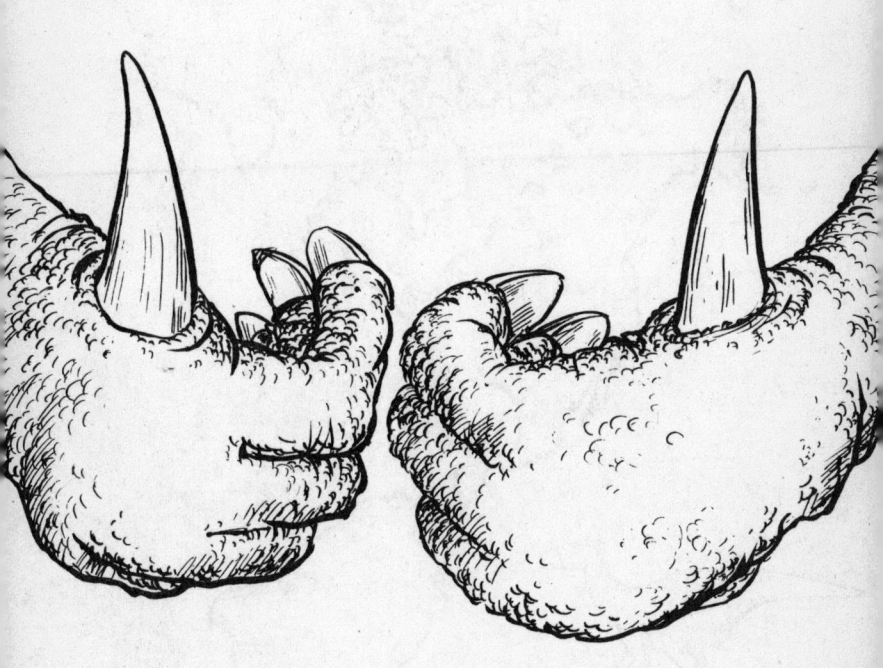

Scientists are finding out new dinosaur facts all the time.

Today, Iguanodon looks different again! Scientists say it had a stiff tail. It held its tail up to balance the rest of its body. It wasn't as big or heavy as early scientists thought, and its bottom wasn't quite so fat!

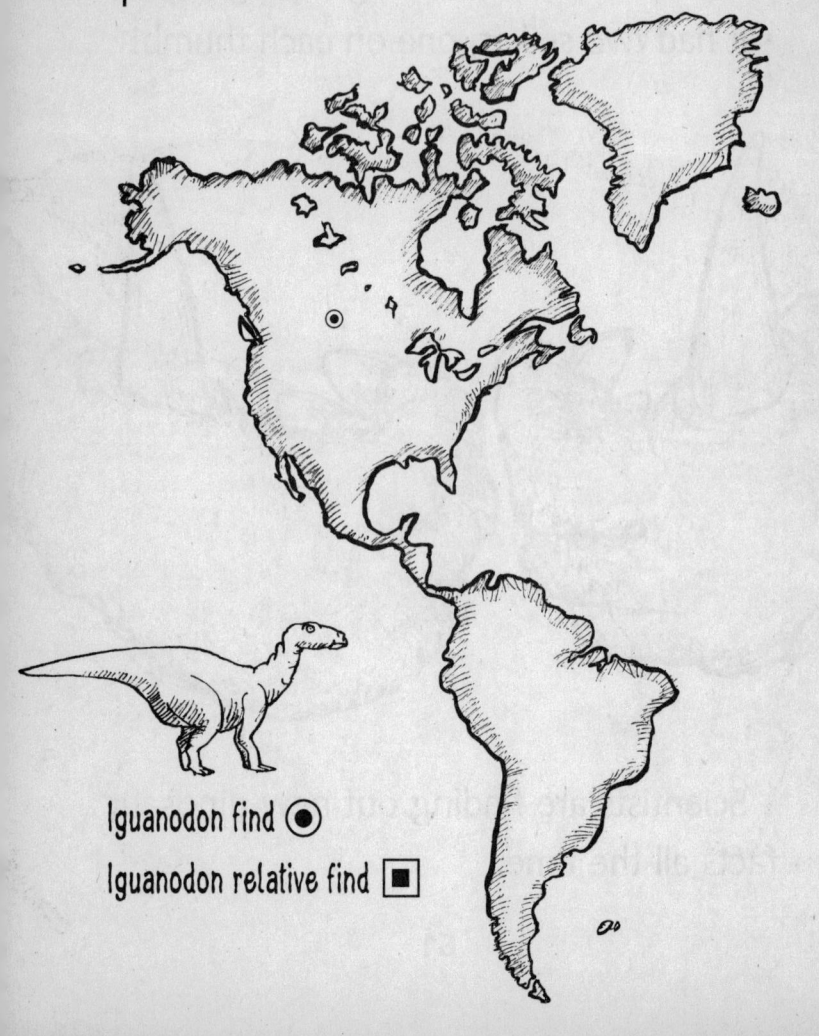

Iguanodon find ◉
Iguanodon relative find ◼

Fossils of Iguanodon and its relatives have been found all over the world. We know more about Iguanodon than most other dinosaurs. That might just prove that Iguanodon was the most successful dinosaur EVER!

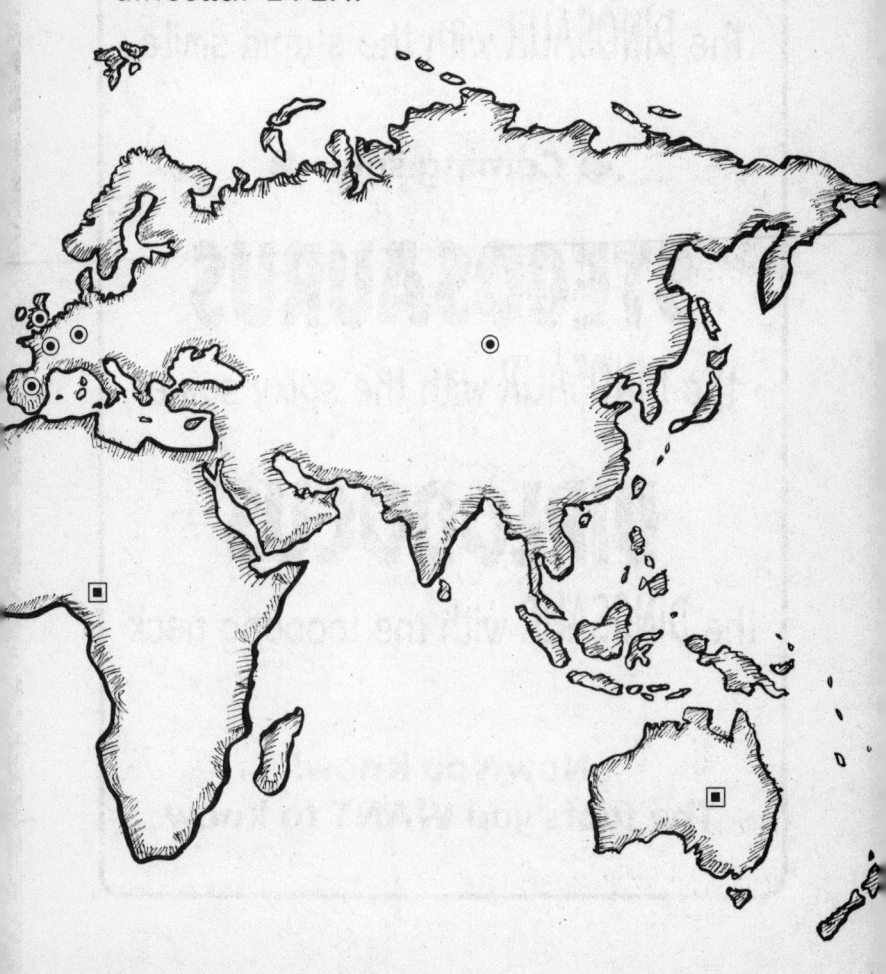

Now you know a lot about Iguanodon, which dinosaur will you discover next?

T.REX
the DINOSAUR with the stupid smile

● **Coming soon** ●

STEGOSAURUS
the DINOSAUR with the spiky spine

DIPLODOCUS
the DINOSAUR with the loooong neck

**Now You Know!
The facts you WANT to know**